Marketing is Warfare

Whether you are a business owner, a marketing manager, or just interested in marketing, you can profit from studying this new version of the ancient guide to competition. For over 2,500 years, *The Art of War* has helped its readers find success using the wisdom of Sun Tzu.

Expressed in an exciting, new way in *The Art of Marketing,* Sun Tzu's immortal ideas tackle our modern form of warfare—market competition. *The Art of Marketing* translates Sun Tzu's lessons to deal with customers, competitors, and the battle for market awareness and position. *The Art of War & The Art of Marketing* together offer you a proven, workable approach to winning the daily battles of the marketplace.

Gary Gagliardi is a highly successful entrepreneur who used Sun Tzu's ancient wisdom to build a multimillion-dollar software company. He has written a number of books about computers, information management and high technology, but he has more recently specialized in writing business books based on the ancient masters. As a longtime student of Sun Tzu, he developed this innovative book for those seeking success.

Buy it today and study it forever!

Books in the Art of Business

Other Books from Clearbridge Publishing

The Art of War: In Sun Tzu's Own Words
The Art of War & The Art of Sales

THE ART OF WAR

&

THE ART OF MARKETING

孫
子
兵
法

To my daughter, Amanda

The Art of War

&

The Art of Marketing

By
Sun Tzu
and
Gary Gagliardi

Clearbridge Publishing

Published by
Clearbridge Publishing

FIRST EDITION
Copyright 1999 © Gary Gagliardi

Clearbridge Publishing and its logo, a transparent bridge, are the trade-marks of Clearbridge Publishing,

Manufactured in the United States of America
Front Cover Art by Gary Gagliardi
Back Cover photograph by Davis Freeman

Library of Congress Catalog Card Number 99-068930
ISBN 1-929194-02-1
Clearbridge Publishing's books may be purchased for business, for any promotional use or for special sales. Please contact:

Clearbridge PUBLISHING
P.O Box 7055, Shoreline, WA 98133
Phone: (206)-533-9357 Fax:(206)-546-9756
www.clearbridge.com
info@clearbridge.com

Contents

Foreword

For over two thousand years, people have preserved and treasured Sun Tzu's famous treatise on war. Today, most readers are not military men, but business people looking for an advantage in market competition. They have discovered that Sun Tzu's lessons can apply well to any struggle for success.

I discovered *The Art of War* over twenty years ago when I was working as a young salesperson. From my first reading, it was clear that Sun Tzu's lessons worked for sales and marketing.

After a successful career in sales, I started my own software company. I rewrote the ancient text to train my sales staff in a book I called *The Art of Sales.* It was received so well that I resolved to write it for a broader audience when I had the chance.

As the head of the company, though, my personal preoccupation was marketing—not just sales. In working with Sun Tzu's text, I couldn't help but see a similarity between his ideas and those in marketing classics such as *Marketing Warfare.* I found Sun Tzu's approach powerful and inspirational. This is the vision that I have tried to capture in the book you are holding, *The Art of Marketing.* I offer this marketing version side-by-side with a complete translation of the original text of *The Art of War.*

As the first of the military classics, *The Art of War* offers a distinct, non-intuitive philosophy on how to discover a winning position and defeat the competition. This philosophy realizes that certain key factors influence the outcome of any confrontation and that victory goes not to the strongest or most aggressive, but to the person who best understands the true situation and what the alternatives are.

In seeing *The Art of War* and *The Art of Marketing* side-by-side, I encourage you read both at the same time. In doing so, I suspect that you can go beyond what I have written and discover your own lessons from the great work. Both works are, by necessity, very general advice. My marketing version is only one possible marketing adaptation of Sun Tzu's lessons. In many sections, I can think of four or five different ways to apply Sun Tzu's words to marketing problems, but I had to choose only one. Few works have the capability of creating as many insights into the ways of the world.

Why should Sun Tzu's philosophy of warfare apply so well to the problems of sales and marketing? It works because all competition arises from the same factors. Sun Tzu wrote about human nature, the issues of confrontation, and what matters in a contest of wills. The nature of competition hasn't changed in the last two thousand years and won't over the next two thousand. The only difference between sales competition, marketing competition, and warfare is the types of tools and the nature of the battleground.

Some have criticized my work with Sun Tzu before reading it because they don't see how anything as horrible as war can teach us useful lessons. More specifically, people see war as an adversarial, destructive process while sales and marketing are cooperative, productive activities. My only defense is to suggest that people read Sun Tzu's work. He did not see warfare as simply a matter of killing the enemy and destroying resources. His goal was convincing the enemy to surrender without a fight. He, more than anyone else, was familiar with the destructive nature of war. He did not teach blood lust. He taught the art of persuasion by another means as an alternative to destruction.

This approach works equally well in the business world. I owe a debt of gratitude to the teachings of Sun Tzu. His lessons helped me throughout my career in sales and perhaps even more in marketing my own products. Adapting his principles, we built our software company into a multimillion-dollar business, doubling in size every few years. His teachings strongly influenced every aspect of our marketing plans. From Sun Tzu, I learned how to discover new markets, how to analyze them, how to target customers, and how to win them from the competition. Within five years, this approach made our product the number one accounting software in our target market.

When we sold our company, I wanted to bring the wisdom of Sun Tzu to a wider audience. I reworked *The Art of Sales* so that it addressed a more general audience interested in selling. After publishing it through Clearbridge earlier this year, I began work on *The Art of Marketing*. If you hear echoes of many other marketing books in *The Art of Marketing*, it is because Sun Tzu has the earlier claim on these concepts. Most marketing people have, at one time or another, studied Sun Tzu.

Originally, I had planned on writing only a sales version and a marketing version of Sun Tzu. I hadn't planned on offering a new translation of *The Art of War* itself and including that translation in my books. In doing my research, however, I discovered that the existing translations disagreed on Sun Tzu's meaning at essential points. I was forced to go back to the Chinese text to faithfully interpret his ideas.

The Internet made it easy to translate the original Chinese characters. Using sites that link the text to Chinese-English dictionaries, I created my own character-by-character translation. This led to my new English translation. Once I saw the character and text versions side-by-side, I decided to offer them together under the title: *The Art of War: In Sun Tzu's Own Words*, also published by Clearbridge. I found that putting *The Art of War* with my sales and marketing adaptations created more interesting works.

As you are reading, notice how closely *The Art of Marketing* follows Sun Tzu's original ideas in *The Art of War*. While *The Art of Marketing* applies Sun Tzu's ideas in ways that he would never have foreseen, it does so respecting the integrity of his thinking. I truly don't think of these marketing ideas as my own, but as interpretations of Sun Tzu's approach to successful competition. I follow his advice and admonitions as closely as possible, line-by-line.

In writing my marketing version, I tried to be as consistent as possible in my translation from the military arena to the business world. Much of this translation was obvious. I simply define marketing as a battle for the customer's mind. The military generals to which Sun Tzu addressed his work become today's business owners and marketing managers. The nation for whom the army fights becomes the company that they are trying to promote. The contested terrain translates into a segment of the marketplace.

What made this interpretation so natural was Sun Tzu's economic view of warfare itself. In the second chapter of *The Art of War*, "Going to War," Sun Tzu reflects on the costly nature of war. The secret to warfare, he concluded, is not just winning battles. It is winning in a way that doesn't impoverish the nation. The goal is to enrich the nation and preserve it. This insight led to his entire approach to war as an exercise in persuasion.

His economic view maps extremely well into any serious thinking about sales and marketing. Our purpose isn't just to win markets, but to do so in a way that profits the company and doesn't bankrupt it in the process. Marketing is, in our era, competition between groups of people for their economic survival. It may be less physically lethal than war, but it is no less serious in terms of the survival of the company and the success of the people involved.

When we make these translations from warfare to marketing competition, the lessons that emerge from Sun Tzu are intriguing.

First, Sun Tzu teaches that winning a market is not enough. The goal is to win easily, with a minimum of cost. In modern terms, the goal is to make a profit in winning. Since marketing is expensive, the goal is to win quickly and efficiently. The most essential ingredient to winning easily is picking your battles. Sun Tzu gives a formula for reasoning out your plan for victory. It looks very like a calculation of profit. You only want to fight for markets in situations where you are certain to win but you also want to be certain that winning is well worth the cost.

Next, his lessons are extremely specific about what to do in certain situations. He wants his readers to pay close attention to the details of their competition. He enumerates different field conditions, different types of competitors, different fatal flaws, different competitive signals, and so on. Although Sun Tzu wrote 2,500 years ago about warfare, when translated to marketing, these detailed lists still look surprisingly complete. Their advice is useful to anyone analyzing their market conditions. People are people. Competition is competition. Winning is winning in every era.

Next, Sun Tzu offers his "cooperative" view of competition. In his eye, you cannot win through your own actions. You don't create successful markets. You can defend your existing situation from loss. You only discover new opportunities when others create them. The secret to your success is recognizing a good market when it presents itself. This may seem like a patient vision of marketing or warfare, but Sun Tzu thought that opportunities were abundant. Every problem creates an opportunity. We just fail to see it.

Finally, Sun Tzu's view of competition is knowledge-intensive. He sees victory going to the person who is the most knowledgeable. He even recognizes creativity as a special and important type of knowledge. In Sun Tzu, there is no substitute for good information. *The Art of War's* last chapter, "Using Spies" makes it clear how essential good information is. In the marketing translation, this chapter becomes "Using Research." These chapters make it clear that Sun Tzu understood the information economy. He clearly saves his most important message for last. He says outright that nothing is as important as acquiring good information.

Despite its relatively short length, this book contains a great deal more specific information than books on marketing two or three times the size. Personally, I have studied *The Art of War* for twenty years. I learn more about sales and marketing every time I read it. I am still discovering new useful interpretations of Sun Tzu's ideas in everyday business activity.

In offering this book, I encourage you to discover your own interpretations of Sun Tzu's ideas for your own business situation. As Sun Tzu almost says, "Creativity is as infinite as the weather and land. It is as inexhaustible as the flow of a river."

Gary Gagliardi, 1999

PLANNING

This is war.
It is the most important skill in the nation.
It is the basis of life and death.
It is the philosophy of survival or destruction.
You must know it well.

Your skill comes from five factors.
Study these factors when you plan war.
You must insist on knowing the nature of:
1. Military philosophy,
2. The weather,
3. The ground,
4. The commander,
5. And military methods.

It starts with your military philosophy.
Command your people in a way that gives them a higher
shared purpose.
You can lead them to death.
You can lead them to life.
They must never fear danger or dishonesty.

MARKET ANALYSIS

This is marketing.
It is the central function of your company.
It is the foundation of fortunes and distress.
Its logic leads to creation and destruction.
You must know how it works.

Five factors decide your success in markets.
Weigh these factors in your market analysis.
You must know:
1. Your marketing philosophy,
2. Your visibility,
3. Your segment,
4. Your capabilities,
5. And the marketing process.

Marketing begins with a philosophy.
When you go to market, you must identify your company's mission.
It must guide you for the long-term.
It must give you a reason to exist.
With a mission, you can overcome obstacles and confusion.

Next, you have the weather.
It can be sunny or overcast.
It can be hot or cold.
It includes the timing of the seasons.

Next is the terrain.
It can be distant or near.
It can be difficult or easy.
It can be open or narrow.
It also determines your life or death.

Next is the commander.
He must be smart, trustworthy, caring, brave and strict.

Finally, you have your military methods.
They include the shape of your organization.
This comes from your management philosophy.
You must master their use.

All five of these factors are critical.
As a commander, you must pay attention to them.
Understanding them brings victory.
Ignoring them means defeat.

Next is your market visibility.
You can be well known or hidden.
You can be popular or overlooked.
Your visibility changes over time.

Next is your target segment.
It can be spread out or be close by.
It can be diverse or specialized.
It can be wide open or just a niche.
Choosing the right market determines success or failure.

Next is your marketing ability.
You must be clever, honest, caring, brave, and disciplined.

Finally, you must have a solid marketing process.
Your organization and channels determine your process.
It also arises from your marketing philosophy.
You must master using a process.

All five of these factors are critical.
You must continuously be aware of them.
Your success requires understanding them.
Overlooking anything leads to failure.

You must learn through planning.
You must question the situation.

You must ask:
Which government has the right philosophy?
Which commander has the skill?
Which season and place has the advantage?
Which method of command works?
Which group of forces has the strength?
Which officers and men have the training?
Which rewards and punishments make sense?
This tells when you will win and when you will lose.
Some commanders perform this analysis.
If you use these commanders, you will win.
Keep them.
Some commanders ignore this analysis.
If you use these commanders, you will lose.
Get rid of them.

Planning gives you an advantage because it makes you listen.
Planning makes you powerful.
Planning makes it easy for you to kill the enemy.
Planning is power.
Planning creates advantages and controls power.

Market analysis reveals what is important to customers.
You need to research many issues.

You must know:
Do you have a workable marketing philosophy?
Does your organization know its segment?
Do you know where and how to contact customers?
Which marketing message will get their attention?
Which issues are important to buyers?
Are your distribution channels properly trained?
What promotions and incentives make sense?
This tells you which customers you can and cannot sell.
You must continually do this market analysis.
If you use it, you will be successful.
Keep at it.
Too many marketing people forget analysis.
If you don't keep it up, you will fail.
The market will reject you.

Analysis forces you to listen to your customers.
Analysis gathers information.
It makes it possible to beat your competition.
Analysis is power.
Analysis exploits your strengths to win dominance.

Warfare is one thing.
It is a philosophy of deception.

When you are ready, you try to appear incapacitated.
When active, you pretend inactivity.
When you are close to the enemy, you appear distant.
When far away, pretend you are near.

If the enemy has strong position, entice him away from it.
If the enemy is confused, be decisive.
If the enemy is solid, prepare against him.
If the enemy is strong, avoid him.
If the enemy is angry, frustrate him.
If the enemy is weaker, make him arrogant.
If the enemy is relaxed, make him work.
If the enemy is united, break him apart.
Attack him when he is unprepared.
Leave when he least expects it.

You will find a place where you can win.
Don't pass it by.

Marketing is focus.
You must control the market's perceptions.

Where you are strong, you must pretend weakness.
Where you focus, you must pretend indifference.
When similar to the competition, emphasize differences.
When you are different, you must appear similar.

Where competition is strong, entice customers away.
Where competition is confused, offer customers leadership.
Where competition is successful, learn from them.
Where competition is entrenched, avoid them.
If your competition is easy to provoke, frustrate them.
If your competition is weak, inflate their threat.
If your competition is easygoing, challenge them to work.
If your competition is united, divide their alliances.
Attack a market when the competition doesn't expect it.
Abandon markets when competition concentrates on them.

You must find market niches where you can win.
Never pass them by.

Before you go to war, you must believe that you can count
on victory.
You must calculate many advantages.
Before you go to battle, you may believe that you can foresee
defeat.
You can count few advantages.
Many advantages add up to victory.
Few advantages add up to defeat.
How can you know your advantages without analyzing them?
We can see where we are by means of our observations.
We can foresee our victory or defeat by planning.

·:●:·

Before entering a market, you must know that you can dominate it.

You must be strong in that particular segment.

Before wasting your resources, you must avoid segments that you cannot dominate.

You don't have enough strength to attack every market.

Dominating segments brings you success.

Struggling in markets brings only failure.

How can you dominate a market without analysis?

You must see where you are by surveying the market.

You can foresee winning the market or losing it by analysis.

Going to War

Everything depends on your use of military philosophy.
Moving the army requires thousands of vehicles.
These vehicles must be loaded thousands of times.
The army must carry a huge supply of arms.
You need ten thousand acres of grain.
This results in internal and external shortages.
Any army consumes resources like an invader.
It uses up glue and paint for wood.
It requires armor for its vehicles.
People complain about the waste of a vast amount of metal.
It will set you back when you raise tens of thousands of
troops.

Using a large army makes war very expensive to win.
Long delays create a dull army and sharp defeats.
Attacking enemy cities drains your forces.
Long campaigns that exhaust the nation's resources are
wrong.

SELECTING A MARKET

Everything depends on your marketing philosophy.
Promoting a company and its products is expensive.
Building market awareness takes thousands of dollars.
You must invent many different approaches.
You need a wealth of resources.
This demands a large investment from your company.
This drains resources from your other operations.
Marketing uses up time and energy.
It demands that you defend your position.
Others complain about how marketing consumes cash.
It takes time to build up the distribution channels that you
require.

Winning a large market is expensive and time consuming.
Delay fatigues your channels and costs you sales.
Attacking entrenched markets drains your resources.
Long marketing campaigns that deplete your company's
resources will fail.

Manage a dull army.
You will suffer sharp defeats.
Drain your forces.
Your money will be used up.
Your rivals multiply as your army collapses and they will
begin against you.
It doesn't matter how smart you are.
You cannot get ahead by taking losses!

You hear of people going to war too quickly.
Still, you won't see a skilled war that lasts a long time.

You can fight a war for a long time or you can make your
nation strong.
You can't do both.

You can never totally understand all the dangers in using
arms.
Therefore, you can never totally understand the advantages
in using arms either.

You want to make good use of war.
Do not raise troops repeatedly.
Do not carry too many supplies.
Choose to be useful to your nation.
Feed off the enemy.
Make your army carry only the provisions it needs.

You can lose the interest of your sales channel.
You then will lose the market.
You can drain your resources.
You will then use up your marketing budget.
As your markets weaken, you inspire your competitors to attack you.
It doesn't matter how smart you think you are.
You can't win a market once you've lost the initiative.

You can sometimes move too fast attacking a market.
However, the slower the attack, the more often you fail.

You can try to play it safe when you go after a market or you can be successful.
You can't have it both ways.

You can never completely insure against failure when you go after a new segment.
You are therefore unlimited in the success that you can achieve from developing new markets.

You want to make good use of your marketing.
Do not change your market focus repeatedly.
Do not try to do too much.
Support the needs of your company.
Feed off your competition.
Do only what you need to do at the moment.

The nation impoverishes itself shipping to troops that are
far away.
Distant transportation is costly for hundreds of families.
Buying goods with the army nearby is also expensive.
These high prices also impoverish hundreds of families.
People quickly exhaust their resources supporting a military
force.
Military forces consume a nation's wealth entirely.
War leaves households in the former heart of the nation with
nothing.

War destroys hundreds of families.
Out of every ten families, war leaves only seven.
War empties the government's storehouses.
Broken armies will get rid of their horses.
They will throw down their armor, helmets, and arrows.
They will lose their swords and shields.
They will leave their wagons without oxen.
War will consume sixty percent of everything you have.

Because of this, the commander's duty is to feed off the
enemy.

Use a cup of the enemy's food.
It is worth twenty of your own.
Win a bushel of the enemy's feed.
It is worth twenty of your own.

You can kill the enemy and frustrate him as well.
Take the enemy's strength from him by stealing away his
supplies.

Marketing to distant areas is costly for you and your company.
Transportation increases the price of what you are selling.
Also, marketing into crowded markets can't be profitable.
This lack of profits can destroy your company.
Most failures result from companies exhausting their resources on marketing.
Media advertising can consume your company entirely.
Marketing can leave the company without profits and worthless.

Many companies have to abandon a market.
Most attempts to win new markets fail.
Failed marketing plans deplete company resources.
Failed marketing forces you to abandon your investments.
You give up the market awareness that you've established.
You must abandon your image and message.
Your distribution is left without support.
Marketing consumes the profits of too many companies.

Because of this, you must go after markets that quickly generate money for your company.

Take a dollar in sales today.
It is worth twenty dollars tomorrow.
Win a dollar in customer sales.
It is worth twenty dollars of market potential.

You must win customers and treat them well.
You need to generate income from your market as soon as possible.

Fight for the enemy's supply wagons.
Capture their supplies by using overwhelming force.
Reward the first who capture them.
Then change their banners and flags.
Mix them in with your own to increase your supply line.
Keep your soldiers strong by providing for them.
This is what it means to beat the enemy while you grow
more powerful.

Make victory in war pay for itself.
Avoid expensive, long campaigns.
The military commander's knowledge is the key.
It determines if the civilian officials can govern.
It determines if the nation's households are peaceful or a
danger to the state.

Marketing must generate more resources.
Win markets that you can easily dominate.
Go after markets where sales are already being made.
Use existing customers to bring in more customers.
Base your promotion on past success in a market.
Your success is what makes you successful.
This is what it means to win a market while growing more influential.

Win markets that pay for themselves.
Avoid expensive, long marketing campaigns.
Knowing your customers is the key.
It determines whether or not your company is well run.
Your marketing determines how difficult or easy it is to build a company.

Planning an Attack

Everyone relies on the arts of war.
A united nation is strong.
A divided nation is weak.
A united army is strong.
A divided army is weak.
A united force is strong.
A divided force is weak.
United men are strong.
Divided men are weak.
A united unit is strong.
A divided unit is weak.

Unity works because it enables you to win every battle you
fight.
Still, this is the foolish goal of a weak leader.
Avoid battle and make the enemy's men surrender.
This is the right goal for a superior leader.

PLANNING A CAMPAIGN

Your business depends on your marketing skills.
A focused campaign works.
An unfocused campaign doesn't.
A single product line is easy to sell.
Many different product lines are hard to sell.
A concentrated effort is successful.
A divided effort fails.
A small market is simple.
A spread-out market is difficult.
A single message works.
Multiple messages don't.

Focus works because it enables you to win every segment you target.
This still doesn't make you a great marketing manager.
You want to win markets without competition.
This is your highest goal.

The best policy is to attack while the enemy is still planning.
The next best is to disrupt alliances.
The next best is to attack the opposing army.
The worst is to attack the enemy's cities.

This is what happens when you attack a city.
You can attempt it, but you can't finish it.
First you must make siege engines.
You need the right equipment and machinery.
You use three months and still cannot win.
Then, you try to encircle the area.
You use three more months without making progress.
The commander still doesn't win and this angers him.
He then tries to swarm the city.
This kills a third of his officers and men.
He still isn't able to draw the enemy out of the city.
This attack is a disaster.

Make good use of war.
Make the enemy's troops surrender.
You can do this fighting only minor battles.
You can draw their men out of their cities.
You can do it with small attacks.
You can destroy the men of a nation.
You must keep your campaign short.

It's best to find markets overlooked by the competition.
The next best is to win away the competition's distributors.
The next best is outmoding the competition's products.
The worst is to attack an entrenched position.

What happens when you attack an entrenched position?
You can campaign, but you cannot win sales.
First, you must prepare the resources needed.
You need to buy advertising and build distribution channels.
This takes months.
You run in circles chasing after the competition.
After more months of work, you still can't get a share.
Management and sales people are impatient for results.
You then try to defame the competition.
This destroys your credibility.
You are still unable to damage their position.
This type of attack is a disaster.

Make good use of marketing.
Let the competition surrender segments to you.
You can do it without a single battle.
You can win customers away from their current suppliers.
You do it by targeting niches.
You can destroy the competition's distribution.
You must move quickly into the market.

You must use total war, fighting with everything you have.
Never stop fighting when at war.
You can gain complete advantage.
To do this, you must plan your strategy of attack.

The rules for making war are:
If you outnumber the enemy ten to one, surround them.
If you outnumber them five to one, attack them.
If you outnumber them two to one, divide them.
If you are equal, then find an advantageous battle.
If you are fewer, defend against them.
If you are much weaker, evade them.

Small forces are not powerful.
However, large forces cannot catch them.

You must master command.
The nation must support you.

Supporting the military makes the nation powerful.
Not supporting the military makes the nation weak.

Politicians create problems for the military in three different
ways.
Ignorant of the army's inability to advance, they order an
advance.
Ignorant of the army's inability to withdraw, they order a
withdrawal.
We call this tying up the army.
Politicians don't understand the army's business.
Still, they think they can run an army.
This confuses the army's officers.

In marketing, you must leverage every resource.
Never stop promoting when you target a segment.
You can gain the advantage if you focus.
To do this, you must plan your marketing strategy.

The rules for winning markets are:
If your distribution is ten times better, dominate a market.
If your distribution is five times better, attack a market.
If your distribution is twice as good, divide the market.
If your distribution is equal, sell only to the best prospects.
If your distribution is weaker, avoid the competition.
If your distribution is much weaker, find market niches.

Small companies cannot sell broad markets.
However, large companies cannot satisfy niche markets.

You must own your own segments.
Your organization must support you.

Focussing on its segments makes a company strong.
Ignoring its segments makes a company weak.

Sales management creates problems in its market in three
different ways.
Ignorant of which segments are winnable, they attack any
market.
Ignorant of which segments cannot be won, they forget
existing markets.
This is called wasting your marketing.
Sales management doesn't understand marketing.
They think that they can go after any market.
This muddles your marketing campaign.

Politicians don't know the army's chain of command.
They give the army too much freedom.
This will create distrust among the army's officers.

The entire army becomes confused and distrusting.
This invites the invasion from many different rivals.
We say correctly that disorder in an army kills victory.

You must know five things to win:
Victory comes from knowing when to attack and when to
avoid battle.
Victory comes from correctly using large and small forces.
Victory comes from everyone sharing the same goals.
Victory comes from finding opportunities in problems.
Victory comes from having a capable commander and the
government leaving him alone.
You must know these five things.
You then know the theory of victory.

We say:
"Know yourself and know your enemy.
You will be safe in every battle.
You may know yourself but not know the enemy.
You will then lose one battle for every one you win.
You may not know yourself or the enemy.
You will then lose every battle."

Sales management doesn't understand market priorities.
They give their sales people too much freedom.
This creates uncertainty in your target market.

If you confuse your target market, you create distrust.
This invites the competition to win away your customers.
An unfocused campaign destroys your chances of success.

You must know five things to win markets.
Success comes from knowing when to invest in a segment
and when to save your money.
You must know how to tackle large markets and small.
Success comes from focussing your company on its market.
Success comes from turning problems into opportunities.
Success comes from market leadership and winning the
trust of sales people.
You must know these five things.
You then know the philosophy of winning markets.

Experience says:
Know your customers and your market.
If you do, you can win any market.
You can know your customers, but not know your segment.
Then, for every sale you make, you will lose another.
You may know neither your customers nor your segment.
Then, you will lose every sale.

POSITIONING

Learn from the history of successful battles.
Your first actions should deny victory to the enemy.
You pay attention to your enemy to find the way to win.
You alone can deny victory to the enemy.
Only your enemy can allow you to win.

You must fight well.
You can prevent the enemy's victory.
You cannot win unless the enemy enables your victory.

We say:
You see the opportunity for victory; you don't create it.

You are sometimes unable to win.
You must then defend.
You will eventually be able to win.
You must then attack.
Defend when you have insufficient strength to win.
Attack when you have more strength than you need to win.

Product Position

Learn from the history of product success.
Redefine the market so that your competition can't win it.
Know the competition so you can deny them victory.
You can use their image to exclude them.
Your competition gives you the opening.

You must campaign well.
You can prevent the enemy's success.
You cannot win without using their position against them.

It is said:
You must find a market; you do not create it.

You cannot always find new markets.
You must then expand your existing markets.
You will eventually be in a position to win new markets.
Then you must go after them.
Stay in your market when you cannot win new ones.
Attack new markets when you are certain to succeed.

You must defend yourself well.
Save your forces and dig in.
You must attack well.
Move your forces when you have a clear advantage.

You must protect your forces until you can completely
triumph.

Some may see how to win.
However, they cannot position their forces where they must.
This demonstrates limited ability.

Some can struggle to a victory and the whole world may
praise their winning.
This also demonstrates a limited ability.

Win as easily as picking up a fallen hair.
Don't use all of your forces.
See the time to move.
Don't try to find something clever.
Hear the clap of thunder.
Don't try to hear something subtle.

Learn from the history of successful battles.
Victory goes to those who make winning easy.
A good battle is one that you will obviously win.
It doesn't take intelligence to win a reputation.
It doesn't take courage to achieve success.

You must defend your markets well.
Conserve your resources and dig in.
You must attack new markets decisively.
Attack them when you find an irresistible position.

Keep yourself in business until you are certain you've found
a great target.

꒐━━

You may see markets that you can win.
Yet you cannot position your products in them.
This shows a limited ability.

You may win a small segment after investing a great deal of
time and resources.
This also shows a limited ability.

Expanding to new markets should be effortless.
Avoid consuming all your resources.
Watch for the time to move.
Don't try to be too clever.
Hearing customers is easy if you listen.
Don't imagine what you want to hear.

Learn from your successful efforts.
Markets go to those who make buying easy.
A good product is one that will obviously create sales.
You are foolish if you just want to get your name known.
Avoid being foolhardy if you want to succeed.

You must win your battles without effort.
Avoid difficult struggles.
Fight when your position must win.
You always win by preventing your defeat.

You must engage only in winning battles.
Position yourself where you cannot lose.
Never waste an opportunity to defeat your enemy.

You win a war by first assuring yourself of victory.
Only afterward do you look for a fight.
Outmaneuver the enemy before the battle and then fight to
win.

You must make good use of war.
Study military philosophy and the art of defense.
You can control your victory or defeat.

This is the art of war.
1. Discuss the distances.
2. Discuss your numbers.
3. Discuss your calculations.
4. Discuss your decisions.
5. Discuss victory.
The ground determines the distance.
The distance determines your numbers.
Your numbers determine your calculations.
Your calculations determine your decisions.
Your decisions determine your victory.

You want to expand without fighting for customers.
Avoid difficult competition.
Redefine products so you are the market leader.
You win buyers by avoiding second place in their minds.

You must invest only in winning campaigns.
Make offers that cannot fail.
Never pass an opportunity to outflank the competition.

You win markets by picking the right targets.
Only then do you invest in the campaign.
You must identify the right market and then campaign to
dominate it.

You must make good use of marketing.
Examine your marketing philosophy and how to defend it
You alone determine your success or failure.

Good marketing requires:
1. A discussion of barriers to entry,
2. A discussion of the needed resources,
3. A discussion of the potential profits,
4. A discussion of your marketing plan,
5. And a discussion of your chances of success.
Customers determine the barriers to entry.
Those barriers determine the needed resources.
Your resources determine the potential profit.
Potential profit determines your marketing plan.
Your marketing plan determines your success.

Creating a winning war is like balancing a coin of gold against
a coin of silver.
Creating a losing war is like balancing coin of a silver against
a coin of gold.

Winning a battle is always a matter of people.
You pour them into battle like a flood of water pouring into
a deep gorge.
This is a matter of positioning.

You want markets when they return more than winning them consumes.

You don't want markets when they cost more to win than they can return.

Winning a campaign depends on picking customers.

When you find the right target customer, your campaign is irresistible.

This is a matter of product positioning.

MOMENTUM

You control a large army as you control a few men.
You just divide their ranks correctly.
You fight a large army the same as you fight a small one.
You only need the right position and communication.
You may meet a large enemy army.
You must be able to encounter the enemy without being
defeated.
You must correctly use both surprise and direct action.
Your army's position must increase your strength.
Troops flanking an enemy can smash them like eggs.
You must correctly use both strength and weakness.

It is the same in all battles.
You use a direct approach to engage the enemy.
You use surprise to win.

You must use surprise for a successful invasion.
Surprise is as infinite as the weather and land.
Surprise is as inexhaustible as the flow of a river.

MARKET MOMENTUM

You attack large markets the same as small ones.
You only need to plan your campaign correctly.
You win large customers the same as you win small ones.
You need the right image and channels.
You may meet larger competitors.
You can compete against them and you should never lose to them.
You only need to use creative and standard approaches.
Together, they increase your momentum in a market.
Attack the competition where they don't expect it.
You must understand both their strengths and weaknesses.

In marketing, every campaign is the same.
You use standard methods to contact the market
You use creativity to win the market.

You must use creativity to be successful in any campaign.
Creativity uses the uniqueness of your position and market.
Creativity never becomes tired or boring.

You can be stopped and yet recover the initiative.
You must use your days and months correctly.

If you are defeated, you can recover.
You must use the four seasons correctly.

There are only a few notes in the scale.
Yet, you can always rearrange them.
You can never hear every song of victory.

There are only a few basic colors.
Yet, you can always mix them.
You can never see all the shades of victory.

There are only a few flavors.
Yet, you can always blend them.
You can never taste all the flavors of victory.

You fight with momentum.
There are only a few types of surprises and direct actions.
Yet, you can always vary the ones you use.
There is no limit in the ways you can win.

Surprise and direct action give birth to each other.
They proceed from each other in an endless cycle.
You can not exhaust all their possible combinations!

Yesterday's failure becomes tomorrow's great success.
You must use your time correctly.

You can make mistakes and still recover.
You can lose one campaign and come back the next.

There are only a few basic marketing techniques.
Yet you can combine them any number of ways.
You can always find a better way to promote your company.

There are only a few basic human needs.
Yet every marketplace feels them differently.
You will never exhaust all the shades of desire.

There are only a few concepts of value.
Yet they change from area to area, moment to moment.
You will never discover all the flavors of worth.

You win markets with momentum.
You only use a few creative and standard techniques.
Yet you can combine them to make each campaign unique.
You have no limit to the ways you can win.

Creative and standard methods require each other.
You must use both and move from one to the other.
Using both, you can never run out of good ideas.

Surging water flows together rapidly.
Its pressure washes away boulders.
This is momentum.

A hawk suddenly strikes a bird.
Its contact alone kills the prey.
This is timing.

You must fight only winning battles.
Your momentum must be overwhelming.
Your timing must be exact.

Your momentum is like the tension of a bent crossbow.
Your timing is like the pulling of a trigger.

War is complicated and confused.
Battle is chaotic.
Nevertheless, you must not allow chaos.

War is sloppy and messy.
Positions turn around.
Nevertheless, you must never be defeated.

Chaos gives birth to control.
Fear gives birth to courage.
Weakness gives birth to strength.

You must control chaos.
This depends on your planning.
Your men must brave their fears.
This depends on their momentum.

Different trends reinforce each other.
Use the force of market trends to wash away resistance.
This is momentum.

You must impact the awareness of the market.
This impact gets attention for your product.
This is timing.

You must only invest in segments that you can win.
Your momentum must be reinforced.
Your timing must be exact.

Your momentum increases the tension in the market.
Your timing should release that tension to create sales.

Markets are always complicated and confused.
Marketing is uncertain.
It is your job to define the market.

Markets are never clear cut and neat.
Positions are constantly changing.
Nevertheless, you must never get lost.

The market's confusion demands your clarity.
The market's uncertainty demands your confidence.
The market's weakness requires your strength.

You must clarify what is confused.
This depends on your analysis.
You must give customers confidence.
This depends on your momentum.

You have strengths and weaknesses.
These come from your position.

You must force the enemy to move to your advantage.
Use your position.
The enemy must follow you.
Surrender a position.
The enemy must take it.
You can offer an advantage to move him.
You can use your men to move him.
You use your strength to hold him.

You want a successful battle.
To do this, you must seek momentum.
Do not just demand a good fight from your people.
You must pick good people and then give them momentum.

You must create momentum.
You create it with your men during battle.
This is comparable to rolling trees and stones.
Trees and stones roll because of their shape and weight.
Offer men safety and they will stay calm.
Endanger them and they will act.
Give them a place and they will hold.
Round them up and they will march.

You make your men powerful in battle with momentum.
This is just like rolling round stones down over a high, steep
cliff.
Use your momentum.

42

You have both strengths and weaknesses.
They arise from your market position.

You must position the competition to your advantage.
Leverage your existing situation.
The competition must adjust to you.
Label the competition in a realistic way.
They must accept that label.
You can change customers' perception of the market.
You can use advertising to form perceptions.
You can use your sales people to reinforce them.

You want to win segment dominance.
You work toward it by building your momentum.
Do not spend money trying to buy a market image.
Find a winning idea that creates momentum in your market.

You must create momentum.
You create it with every aspect of your campaign.
Everything should flow together easily.
Things flow together because of their logic and weight.
Offer a market safety and they will stay with you.
Scare a market with danger and they will adapt.
Give them a vision they can hold on to.
Get the market moving and they will follow you.

You make yourself powerful in a market with momentum.
People follow other people like water pouring over a high cliff.
Use momentum.

Weakness and Strength

Always arrive first to the empty battlefield to await the
enemy at your leisure.
If you are late and hurry to the battlefield, fighting is more
difficult.

You want a successful battle.
Move your men, but not into opposing forces.

You can make the enemy come to you.
Offer him an advantage.
You can make the enemy avoid coming to you.
Threaten him with danger.

When the enemy is fresh, you can tire him.
When he is well fed, you can starve him.
When he is relaxed, you can move him.

NEED AND SATISFACTION

You want the advantage of getting to the market before the competition does.
Avoid attacking segments where the competition is already entrenched.

Your only goal is to dominate your market.
Find new segments; don't follow the competition.

You can make customers come to you.
Entice them with unique offerings.
You can stop the competition from copying you.
Pick an offering that is dangerous for them.

If the market is comfortable, make it uncomfortable.
If the market is satisfied, make it hungry for more.
If the market is lethargic, make it react.

Leave any place without haste.
Hurry to where you are unexpected.
You can easily march hundreds of miles without tiring.
To do so, travel through areas that are deserted.
You must take whatever you attack.
Attack when there is no defense.
You must have walls to defend.
Defend where it is impossible to attack.

Be skilled in attacking.
Give the enemy no idea of where to defend.

Be skillful in your defense.
Give the enemy no idea of where to attack.

Be subtle! Be subtle!
Arrive without any clear formation.
Quietly! Quietly!
Arrive without a sound.
You must use all your skill to control the enemy's decisions.

Advance where they can't defend.
Charge through their openings.
Withdraw where the enemy cannot chase you.
Move quickly so that they cannot catch you.

Abandon any established position gradually.
Quickly stake out new segments before the competition.
You can move quickly with no competition.
To do so, you must find unexplored areas.
You must dominate any market you go after.
You do this by finding unsatisfied needs.
You must hold the markets that you have won.
You must leave no needs for your competition to satisfy.

You must be skilled in winning markets.
Find needs that the competition has overlooked.

You must be skilled in keeping markets.
Leave no unmet needs for the competition to exploit.

You must change your marketing carefully.
Don't let the competition know your plan.
You must keep quiet within your industry.
Move into new segments quietly.
You must skillfully control competition's perception.

Make markets where customers need you.
Aggressively fill the gaps in the market.
Shelter in markets where there are barriers to entry.
Move quickly so that the competition cannot copy you.

I always pick my own battles.
The enemy can hide behind high walls and deep trenches.
I do not try to win by fighting him directly.
Instead, I attack a place that he must rescue.
I avoid the battles that I don't want.
I can divide the ground and yet defend it.
I don't give the enemy anything to win.
Divert him from coming to where you defend.

I make their men take a position while I take none.
I then focus my forces where the enemy divides his forces.
Where I focus, I unite my forces.
When the enemy divides, he creates many small groups.
I want my large group to attack one of his small ones.
Then I have many men where the enemy has but a few.
My large force can overwhelm his small one.
I then go on to the next small enemy group.
I will take them one at a time.

We must keep the place that we've chosen as a battleground
a secret.
The enemy must not know.
Force the enemy to prepare his defense in many places.
I want the enemy to defend many places.
Then I can choose where to fight.
His forces will be weak there.

You must target your own market.
Your competitors are well entrenched.
You can't beat them by attacking them directly.
Instead, find a new segment they don't have.
Avoid competition that you cannot beat.
You can find a segment that you can own.
Don't leave the competition any share to win.
Distract them from coming after your customers.

See where the competition is before you move.
Focus on the gaps in the competition's efforts.
When you focus, you concentrate your energies.
When competition divides their attention, they create needs.
You must focus your efforts on unmet needs.
You can dominate in a segment that others overlook.
You can easily beat the competition in your segment.
You then must move on to the next neglected segment.
Tackle them one at a time.

You must keep your market focus a secret from the
competition.
Your competition must never guess it.
Force them to defend against you in every possible area.
They must spread themselves too thin.
You can choose the segment you want.
They will be weak there.

If he reinforces his front lines, he depletes his rear.
If he reinforces his rear, he depletes his front.
If he reinforces his right, he depletes his left.
If he reinforces his left, he depletes his right.
Without knowing the place of attack, he cannot prepare.
Without a place, he will be weak everywhere.

The enemy has weak points.
Prepare your men against them.
He has strong points.
Make his men prepare themselves against you.

You must know the battle ground.
You must know the time of battle.
You can then travel a thousand miles and still win the battle.

The enemy should not know the battleground.
He shouldn't know the time of battle.
His left will be unable to support his right.
His right will be unable to support his left.
His front lines will be unable to support his rear.
His rear will be unable to support his front.
His support is distant even if it is only ten miles away.
What unknown place can be close?

We control the balance of forces.
The enemy may have many men but they are superfluous.
How can they help him to victory?

If the competition focuses on price, they sacrifice quality.
If they focus on quality, they are vulnerable on price.
If they focus on quickness, they will lack accuracy.
If they focus on accuracy, they lose on quickness.
Without knowing your focus, they cannot fight you directly.
If they claim every advantage, they are weak everywhere.

Markets have unmet needs.
You must prepare to address them.
The competition can satisfy some customers.
Make them spread themselves to thinly.

You must know exactly what your focus is.
You must time your campaign precisely.
No matter how difficult the market, you can capture it.

Your competition must not know your point of attack.
They must never know when you plan to move.
If the competition's market is global, yours is local.
If they sell to everyone, you can specialize.
If they sell to large companies, you can target small ones.
If they sell to households, you can sell to businesses.
They miss your market even if their offices are next-door.
If they don't know your target, how can they fight you?

You decide the balance of power when you pick a segment.
Competitors may have more resources, but not there.
How can their size hurt you?

We say:
You must let victory happen.

The enemy may have many men.
You can still control him without a fight.

When you form your strategy, know the strengths and
weaknesses of your plan.
When you execute, know how to manage both action and
inaction.
When you take a position, know the deadly and the winning
grounds.
When you battle, know when you have too many or too few
men.

Use your position as your war's centerpiece.
Arrive at the battle without a formation.
Don't take a position.
Then even the best spies can't report it.
Even the wisest general cannot plan to counter you.
Take a position where you can triumph using superior
numbers.
Keep the enemy's forces ignorant.
Their troops will learn of my location when my position will
win.
They must not know how our location gives us a winning
position.
Make the battle one from which they cannot recover.
You must always adjust your position to their position.

It is said:
You must permit yourself to be successful.

The competition may be much more powerful.
You can still control them by avoiding a confrontation.

When you shape a market strategy, know its strengths and weaknesses.
When you attack a market, know what needs to be done and what doesn't.
When you position your product, know where people are satisfied and where they have needs.
When you compete, know when you have the advantage and when you are overmatched.

Use your product position to leverage your campaign.
Don't attack new markets with a me-too image.
Be mysterious.
Then the competition cannot copy you.
You can beat anyone if they don't know what to expect.
Go after segments when you can become the dominant player.
Keep your competition in the dark.
They should only learn your target when you develop a winning position.
They should not know how you became so strong in any particular market.
Make sure that they cannot steal the market back from you.
Copy any moves they make to try to win it back.

Manage your military position like water.
Water takes every shape.
It avoids the high and moves to the low.
Your war can take any shape.
It must avoid the strong and strike the weak.
Water follows the shape of the land that directs its flow.
Your forces follow the enemy who determines how you win.

Make war without a standard approach.
Water has no consistent shape.
If you follow the enemy's shifts and changes, you can always
win.
We call this shadowing.

Fight five different campaigns without a firm rule for victory.
Use all four seasons without a consistent position.
Your timing must be sudden.
A few weeks determine your failure or success.

You must remain fluid in your positioning.
Like liquid, you can take any shape.
You start where there are the most profits and then spread.
You can adjust to any situation.
You must avoid strength and attack people's needs.
Communication shapes the market and directs its flow.
You find your market and let it direct your actions.

You must avoid rigid marketing plans.
Ideas have no consistent shape.
You win markets by following the competition and adapting to their openings.
This is called shadowing.

Use different tactics: no single approach always wins.
No specific timing and no single message will always work.
You must always create a sense of urgency.
An instant may determine your success or failure.

ARMED CONFLICT

Everyone uses the arts of war.
You accept orders from the government.
Then you assemble your army.
You organize your men and build camps.
You must avoid disasters from armed conflict.

Seeking armed conflict can be disastrous.
Because of this, a detour can be the shortest path.
Because of this, problems can become opportunities.

Use an indirect route as your highway.
Use the search for advantage to guide you.
When you fall behind, you must catch up.
When you get ahead, you must wait.
You must know the detour that most directly accomplishes
your plan.

Undertake armed conflict when you have an advantage.
Seeking armed conflict for its own sake is dangerous.

MARKETING CONTACT

Everyone uses the art of marketing.
You get your direction from the company.
Then you put together your plans.
You prioritize your tasks and targets.
You must avoid mistakes in contacting the market.

Market contact is costly and dangerous.
Because of this, you must look for shortcuts.
You must find the opportunity hidden in every problem.

You must find different channels of distribution.
Let your quest for customers guide you.
If customers are ahead of you, you must catch up.
If you are ahead of the market, you must wait for it.
You must know how to generate real sales through your plan.

Only make marketing contact when you're ready to sell.
Marketing contact for its own sake is dangerous.

You can build up an army to fight for an advantage.
Then you won't catch the enemy.
You can force your army to go fight for an advantage.
Then you abandon your heavy supply wagons.

You keep only your armor and hurry straight after the
enemy.
You avoid stopping day or night.
You use many roads at the same time.
You go hundreds of miles to fight for an advantage.
Then the enemy catches your commanders and your army.
Your strong soldiers get there first.
Your weaker soldiers follow behind.
Using this approach, only one in ten will arrive.
You can try to go fifty miles to fight for an advantage.
Then your commanders and army will stumble.
Using this method, only half of your soldiers will make it.
You can try to go thirty miles to fight for an advantage.
Then only two out of three get there.

If you make your army travel without good supply lines, they
will die.
Without supplies and food, your army will die.
If you don't save the harvest, your army will die.

You can slowly build a campaign to fight for a position.
Then the competition will beat you.
You can rush into a market to beat the competition.
You then fail to build distribution channels.

You can develop your message and rush straight after notoriety.
You can work day and night.
You can promote through every channel.
You can go everywhere to get your name known.
Then the competition captures your customers and sales.
Your message gets there first.
Your ability to sell lags behind.
Only a small fraction of your efforts will result in sales.
You can try marketing only a little ahead of distribution.
You will make mistakes in filling orders.
You will only capture half your market.
You can try to stretch your sales force too thin.
You will still only win two out of three sales.

If you try to market without good distribution, your campaign will fail.
Without sales and shipping, your campaign will fail.
Without managing your resources, your campaign will fail.

Do not let any of your potential enemies know of what you
are planning.
You must stay with the enemy.
You must know the lay of the land.
You must know where the obstructions are.
You must know where the marshes are.
If you don't, you cannot move the army.
You must use local guides.
If you don't, you can't take advantage of the terrain.

You make war using a deceptive position.
If you use deception, then you can move.
Using deception, you can upset the enemy and change the
situation.
You must move as quickly as the wind.
You must rise like the forest.
You must invade and plunder like fire.
You must stay as motionless as a mountain.
You must be as mysterious as the fog.
You must strike like sounding thunder.

Divide your troops to plunder the villages.
When on open ground, dividing is an advantage.
Don't worry about organization, just move.
Be the first to find a new route that leads directly to a
winning plan.
This is the how you are successful at armed conflict.

Instead, you must initially keep quiet about where you are planning to sell.
You must match the distribution of the competition.
You must know your market and its customers.
You must know where the potential problems are.
You must avoid bogging down in logistics.
If you don't, you can't move your products.
You must rely on proven service providers.
If you don't, you won't get the advantage of the market.

You must disguise your intentions in the market.
Using surprise, you can make easy progress.
Using surprise, you can interest customers and confuse the competition.
You must keep your campaign light and swift.
You must stand up and be noticed.
You must go after orders and win sales.
You must be solid and patient.
You must be shadowy and mysterious.
You must be bold and courageous.

Use half of your efforts to close sales with customers.
When the market is open, multiple channels work.
Don't worry about organization; just get sales.
Being the first to invent a new sales approach creates a winning campaign.
This is the how you are successful at marketing contact.

Military experience says:
"You can speak, but you will not be heard.
You must use gongs and drums.
You cannot really see your forces just by looking.
You must use banners and flags."

You must master gongs, drums, banners and flags.
Place people as a single unit where they can all see and hear.
You must unite them as one.
Then, the brave cannot advance alone.
The fearful cannot withdraw alone.
You must force them to act as a group.

In night battles, you must use numerous fires and drums.
In day battles, you must use many banners and flags.
You must position your people to control what they see and
hear.

You control your army by controlling its emotions.
As a general, you must be able to control emotions.

In the morning, a person's energy is high.
During the day, it fades.
By evening, a person's thoughts turn to home.
You must use your troops wisely.
Avoid the enemy's high spirits.
Strike when they are lazy and want to go home.
This is how you master energy.

Experience in marketing teaches us:
"You can advertise, but you will not be heard.
You must get people's attention.
You cannot be seen just by having a presence.
Use showmanship and magic."

Use gimmicks, games, and showmanship to get the market's attention.
Tie your campaign together.
Do not offer novel concepts alone.
Tie them with comfortable, familiar ideas.
Every idea must amplify a single, clear message.

When unknown, you must create excitement and interest.
If you are better known, you still must keep it engaging.
You must take a position that everyone can see and appreciate.

ο—★

You must get the market's attention.
In marketing, you must generate emotions.

Early in the campaign, market resistance is high.
As time goes on, resistance fades.
By the end, people want security.
You must use your timing wisely.
Avoid tough resistance.
Sell when resistance fades and buyers want security.
This is how you master the energy of others.

Use discipline to await the chaos of battle.
Keep relaxed to await a crisis.
This is how you master emotion.

Stay close to home to await a distant enemy.
Stay comfortable to await the weary enemy.
Stay well fed to await the hungry enemy.
This is how you master power.

Don't entice the enemy when their ranks are orderly.
You must not attack when their formations are solid
This is how you master adaptation.
You must follow these military rules.
Do not take a position facing the high ground.
Do not oppose those with their backs to wall.
Do not follow those who pretend to flee.
Do not attack the enemy's strongest men.
Do not swallow the enemy's bait.
Do not block an army that is heading home.
Leave an escape outlet for a surrounded army.
Do not press a desperate foe.
This is the art of war.

Keep organized to face the problems raised by marketing.
Keep calm and patient in a crisis.
This is how you master your own emotions.

Hold your ground and await a drifting market.
Stay positive and await a wavering market.
Keep successful and await a needy market.
This is how you master power.

Do not attack markets where the competition is orderly.
You must not attack where their organization is solid.
This is how you master adapting.
You must follow these marketing rules:
Do not take a position against strong prejudices.
Do not forget to give buyers a choice.
Do not duplicate messages others seem to abandon.
Do not target the competition's strongest offering.
Do not believe everything that research tells you.
Do not block the customer from buying.
Give the customer a choice to make.
Do not force a hasty decision.
These are the rules of marketing.

ADAPTABILITY

Everyone uses the arts of war.
As a general, you get your orders from the government.
You gather your troops.
On dangerous ground, you must not camp.
Where the roads intersect, you must join your allies.
When an area is cut off, you must not delay in it.
When you are surrounded, you must scheme.
In a life-of-death situation, you must fight.
There are roads that you must not take.
There are armies that you must not fight.
There are strongholds that you must not attack.
There are positions that you must not defend.
There are government commands that must not be obeyed.

Military leaders must be experts in knowing how to adapt to
win.
This will teach you the use of war.

Adapting to Market Conditions

These are basic rules of marketing.
You get your direction from your company.
You organize your marketing campaign.
Where conditions are impossible, move on.
Where alliances are needed, you must find partners.
When a market leads nowhere, you must avoid it
When you are outmaneuvered, you must get creative.
When you are in a do-or-die situation, you must win.
There are channels that you must avoid.
There are segments that you don't want.
There are competitors that you cannot challenge.
There are positions that you cannot defend.
There are times when you ignore all the rules.

You must become an expert at knowing how to adapt to
win your market.
Adapting to the situation is the key to success.

Some commanders are not good at making adjustments to
find an advantage.
They can know the shape of the terrain.
Still, they can not find an advantageous position.

Some military commanders do not know how to adjust their
methods.
They can find an advantageous position.
Still, they can not use their men effectively.

You must be creative in your planning.
You must adapt to your opportunities and weaknesses.
You can use a variety of approaches and still have a
consistent result.
You must adjust to a variety of problems and consistently
solve them.

You can deter your potential enemy by using his weaknesses
against him.
You can keep your enemy's army busy by giving it work to
do.
You can rush your enemy by offering him an advantageous
position.

Some marketers are unable to change their approach to fit a given situation.
They might know the conditions in the market.
Still, they are unable to discover the right position.

Some marketers attempt to sell without changing their usual approach.
They can figure out what the right position is.
Still, they are unable to adapt so they can use it.

You must be inventive in creating your marketing plan.
You can find strengths and weaknesses in every situation.
You can use different messages and still consistently win markets.
Every market offers unique problems, but you can always find good solutions.

You can win any market by using its own weaknesses against it.
You must engage customers by forcing them to think about their situation.
You can speed the marketing process by offering them unique benefits.

You must make use of war.
Do not trust that the enemy isn't coming.
Trust on your readiness to meet him.
Do not trust that the enemy won't attack.
We must rely only on our ability to pick a place that the
enemy can't attack.

You can exploit five different faults in a leader.
If he is willing to die, you can kill him.
If he wants to survive, you can capture him.
He may have a quick temper.
You can then provoke him with insults.
If he has a delicate sense of honor, you can disgrace him.
If he loves his people, you can create problems for him.
In every situation, look for these five weaknesses.
They are common faults in commanders.
They always lead to military disaster.

To overturn an army, you must kill its general.
To do this, you must use these five weaknesses.
You must always look for them.

You must use your resources carefully.
Do not expect to win any market without resistance.
Instead, be ready to meet resistance.
Do not trust that competitors won't attack you.
Instead, position your company so that others can't easily attack it.

All marketing organizations have five potential flaws.
If they are willing to lose a market, they will lose it.
If they lack courage, they can be scared away.
Some marketing organizations overreact.
You can provoke them into mistakes.
If they are open to criticism, you can embarrass them.
If they love their products, you can challenge them.
In every situation, look for these five weaknesses.
They are common faults in any company's marketing.
They can lead you to market disaster.

These weaknesses can destroy you and your campaign.
You must know how to exploit them in others.
You must always be aware of them.

ARMED MARCH

Everyone moving their army must adjust to the enemy.

Keep out of the mountains and in the valleys.
Position yourself on the heights facing the sun.
To win your battles, never attack uphill.
This is how you position your army in the mountains.

When water blocks you, keep far away from it.
Let the enemy cross the river and wait for him.
Do not meet him in midstream.
Wait for him to get half his forces across and then take
advantage of the situation.

You need to be able to fight.
You can't do that if you are in the water when you meet an
attack.
Position yourself upstream, facing the sun.
Never face against the current.
Always position your army upstream when near the water.

THE MARKETING CAMPAIGN

In every marketing campaign, you adjust to the customer.

Keep the cost affordable and avoid the highest prices.
Position yourself above the competition and get attention.
To win the market, never attack a more costly product.
This is how to position yourself in price markets.

If the media is hostile to you, avoid them.
Let your competition tangle with the press.
Don't battle competition in the media.
Wait for the media to attack them, then take advantage of
the situation.

You need to generate sales.
You can't sell if you are battling the press when the
competition attacks you.
Position yourself in a favorable light with the media.
Never try to fight them.
Always play to their prejudices when dealing with them.

You may have to move across marshes.
Move through them quickly without stopping.
You may meet the enemy in the middle of a marsh.
You must keep on the water grasses.
Keep your back to a clump of trees.
This is how you position your army in a marsh.

On a level plateau, take a position that you can change.
Keep the higher ground on your right and to the rear.
Keep the danger in front of you and safety behind.
This is how you position yourself on a level plateau.

You can find an advantage in all four of these situations.
Learn from the great emperor who used positioning to
conquer his four rivals.

Armies are stronger on high ground and weaker on low.
They are better camping on sunny, southern hillsides than on
the shady, northern ones.
Provide for your army's health and place it well.
Your army will be free from disease.
Done correctly, this means victory.

You must sometimes defend on a hill or riverbank.
You must keep on the south side in the sun.
Keep the uphill slope at your right rear.

This will give the advantage to your army.
It will always give you a position of strength.

You may have to win a weak segment.
Win them quickly and move to a stronger one.
You may meet competition in a weak segment.
If you do, stay with the top companies in that group.
Defend your position with these companies.
This is how you position yourself in weak segments.

In broad markets, keep your marketing flexible.
Offer a high quality product and get attention.
Stay in front of the competition and avoid missteps.
This is how to position yourself in broad markets.

You can find an advantage in any market.
Learn from past market leaders who have found success in
their markets.

Marketing is stronger with high goals and weaker with low.
You are better staking out a high, visible goal than in a low,
secretive one.
Keep your organization strong by giving it a mission.
Your organization will be free from cynicism.
Do this correctly and it will win you markets.

Sometimes you must defend a higher price.
Make the better value of your product known.
You always want the best value supporting you.

Quality will always give an advantage to your campaign.
It will always give you a position of strength.

Stop the march when the rain swells the river into rapids.
You may want to ford the river.
Wait until it subsides.

All regions have dead-ends such as waterfalls.
There are deep lakes.
There are high cliffs.
There are dense jungles.
There are thick quagmires.
There are steep crevasses.
Get away from all these quickly.
Do not get close to them.
Keep them at a distance.
Maneuver the enemy close to them.
Position yourself facing these dangers.
Push the enemy back into them.

Danger can hide on your army's flank.
There are reservoirs and lakes.
There are reeds and thickets.
There are forests of trees.
Their dense vegetation provides a hiding place.
You must cautiously search through them.
They can always hide an ambush.

Stop the campaign when the market news is in a furor.
You may want to use the press.
Wait until the furor subsides.

All markets have barriers to entry.
There are knowledge issues.
There are cost issues.
There are distribution issues.
There are legal issues.
There are volume issues.
Get past them quickly.
Circumvent them in your campaign.
Don't let them become problems.
Let your competition struggle with them.
Keep your eye on these problems.
Let your competitors be surprised by them.

Danger can hide at the edges of your market.
Beware of habits and prejudices.
Beware of making false assumptions.
Beware of market influences.
They can provide a secret base for competitive attack.
You must carefully research the market.
You don't want to be surprised.

Sometimes, the enemy is close by but remains calm.
Expect to find him in a natural stronghold.
Other times, he remains at a distance but provokes battle.
He wants you to attack him.

He sometimes shifts the position of his camp.
He is looking for an advantageous position.

The trees in the forest move.
Expect that the enemy is coming.
The tall grasses obstruct your view.
Be suspicious.

The birds take flight.
Expect that the enemy is hiding.
Animals startle.
Expect an ambush.

Notice the dust.
It sometimes rises high in a straight line.
Vehicles are coming.
The dust appears low in a wide band.
Foot soldiers are coming.
The dust seems scattered in different areas.
The enemy is collecting firewood.
Any dust is light and settling down.
The enemy is setting up camp.

If competition sells to your marketplace but are quiet,
You should expect that they have a strong position.
If competition distances itself from you but threatens,
They plan to attack your position.

If the competition's position seems to invite attack,
Always expect that they have a secret advantage.

If opinions in the market begin to shift,
Expect that the competition is active.
If the market is difficult to evaluate,
Expect to be surprised once you are in it.

If market consultants are suddenly quiet,
Suspect that the competition is sharing a secret.
If buyers suddenly bolt,
The competitor is undercutting you.

Ask for information about the competition.
When news comes from market leaders and consultants,
Expect a quick, direct marketing campaign against you.
When news comes from everywhere in the market,
This means that they have many sales people active.
If news of the competition is scattered in different areas,
This means that they are researching the market.
If news of the competition becomes rarer and rarer,
This means that they are waiting.

Your enemy speaks humbly while building up forces.
He is planning to advance.

The enemy talks aggressively and pushes as if to advance.
He is planning to retreat.

Small vehicles exit his camp first and move to positions on
the army's flanks.
They are forming a battle line.

Your enemy tries to sue for peace but without offering a
treaty.
He is plotting.

Your enemy's men run to leave and yet form ranks.
You should expect action.

Half his army advances and the other half retreats.
He is luring you.

Your enemy plans to fight but his men just stand there.
They are starving.

Those who draw water drink it first.
They are thirsty.

Your enemy sees an advantage but does not advance.
His men are tired.

Birds gather.
Your enemy has abandoned his camp.

If competitive marketing is limited but growing,
Prepare for a full campaign.

If competition claims to target you but only feigns attack,
Expect them to give up.

If the competition advertises against you in a way that
supports a sales effort,
They are serious about winning your customers.

If your competitors offer to surrender a segment without
anything in return,
Expect them to double cross you.

If the competition withdraws but organizes their sales force,
Expect them to come back again.

If some competition leaves a market while others go after it,
Don't be lured into it.

If competition targets a market, but is idle;
They are out of resources.

If competition pays salespeople to collect payments,
They are short of money.

If competition has more opportunity but does nothing,
They are too busy to do more.

If market leaders and consultants come to you,
Your competitor has abandoned the marketplace.

Your enemy's soldiers call in the night.
They are afraid.

Your enemy's army is raucous.
They do not take their commander seriously.

Your enemy's banners and flags shift.
Order is breaking down.

Your enemy's officers are irritable.
They are exhausted.

Your enemy's men kill their horses for meat.
They are out of provisions.

They don't put their pots away or return to their tents.
They expect to fight to the death.

Enemy troops appear sincere and agreeable.
But their men are slow to speak to each other.
They are no longer united.

Your enemy offers too many incentives to his men.
He is in trouble.

Your enemy gives out too many punishments.
His men are weary.

Your enemy first attacks and then is afraid of your larger
force.
His best troops have not arrived.

If competitors secretly ask you for information,
They are confused.

If the competition's salespeople are undisciplined,
They don't take their company's management seriously.

If competition suddenly changes their message and image,
They are falling into chaos.

If the competition's top management is easily angered,
They are stretched thin.

If your competitors suspend their advertising,
They are short of funds.

If competitors abandon the niceties and politeness,
Expect them to fight you to the end.

The competition's allies seem friendly with each other.
Nevertheless, they are slow to communicate.
They are no longer together.

If the competition offers too many incentives to buy,
They are in trouble.

Your competitor tightens their sales terms;
They are under pressure.

Your competitors first attack you and then quickly withdraw
from your market.
They are developing more resources.

Your enemy comes in a conciliatory manner.
He needs to rest and recuperate.

Your enemy is angry and appears to welcome battle.
This goes on for a long time, but he doesn't attack.
He also doesn't leave the field.
You must watch him carefully.

If you are too weak to fight, you must find more men.
In this situation, you must not act aggressively.
You must unite your forces, expect the enemy, recruit men
and wait.

You must be cautious about making plans and adjust to the
enemy.
You must increase the size of your forces.

With new, undedicated soldiers, you can depend on them if
you discipline them.
They will tend to disobey your orders.
If they do not obey your orders, they will be useless.

You can depend on seasoned, dedicated soldiers.
But you must avoid disciplining them without reason.
Otherwise, you cannot use them.

You must control your soldiers with *esprit de corp*.
You must bring them together by winning victories.
You must get them to believe in you.

The competition suggests a partnership with you.
They are simply buying time.

The competition sounds aggressive but does not campaign.
They remain in the market without attacking you.
They never withdraw from the market either.
You must keep your eye on them.

If your distribution channels are weak, you can build them.
However, you must not campaign for a market.
You must consolidate your position, prepare for the
competition, and take your time.

You must plan carefully and never take your competitors
lightly.
You must grow your markets.

With new sales channels, you must be consistent in your
programs.
Otherwise, they will get confused.
If they are confused, you have no control.

It is different with established distribution channels.
You must show flexibility.
They serve you best by giving you new ideas.

You control your sales channels through market interest.
You must win them over by generating sales through them.
They must believe you are valuable.

Make it easy for them to obey your orders by training your
people.
Your people will then obey you.
If you do not make it easy to obey, you won't train your
people.
Then they will not obey.

Make your commands easy to follow.
You must understand the way a crowd thinks.

Make it easy for sales people to sell for you by educating them.
They will then follow your direction.
If you make offerings too complex, you won't be able to train sales people.
They will stop listening to you.

You must make your offering easy to understand.
You must understand how groups of people think.

FIELD POSITION

Some field positions are unobstructed.
Some field positions are entangling.
Some field positions are supporting.
Some field positions are constricted.
Some field positions give you a barricade.
Some field positions are spread out.

You can attack from some positions easily.
Others can attack you easily as well.
We call these unobstructed positions.
These positions are open.
On them, be the first to occupy a high, sunny area.
Put yourself where you can defend your supply routes.
Then you will have an advantage.

MARKET POSITION

Some market positions are open.
Some market positions are tricky.
Some market positions are entrenched.
Some market positions are exclusive.
Some market positions are easy to protect.
Some market positions are unfocused.

You can market from some positions easily.
Others can attack you easily as well.
These are open market positions.
These positions present no barriers.
With these positions, seek well-publicized market wins.
Concentrate on generating sales and cash.
They are then strong positions.

You can attack from some positions easily.
Disaster arises when you try to return to them.
These are entangling positions.
These field positions are one-sided.
Wait until your enemy is unprepared.
You can then attack from these positions and win.
Avoid a well prepared enemy.
You will try to attack and lose.
Since you can't return, you will meet disaster.
These field positions offer no advantage.

I cannot leave some positions without losing an advantage.
If the enemy leaves this ground, he also loses an advantage.
We call these supporting field positions.
These positions strengthen you.
The enemy may try to entice me away.
Still, I will hold my position.
You must entice the enemy to leave.
You then strike him as he is leaving.
These field positions offer an advantage.

Some field positions are constricted.
I try to get to these positions before the enemy does.
You must fill these areas and await the enemy.
Sometimes, the enemy will reach them first.
If he fills them, do not follow him.
But if he fails to fill them, you can go after him.

You can campaign from some positions easily.
You cannot go back to them after striking out.
These are tricky positions.
They give you one chance.
Wait until the competition is vulnerable.
You can then use these positions to win their business
Avoid using these positions against strong competition.
You will launch your campaign and fail.
Since you can't retrench, you lose your only chance.
These positions offer no real advantage.

You cannot shift from some positions without losing.
If your competition shifts, they will lose as well.
These are entrenched market positions.
Know when your market position is entrenched.
The competition may try to lure you away.
You must hold your position.
You must tempt the competition to try something new.
You can then attack them.
Entrenched positions offer an advantage.

Some market positions are exclusive.
You must establish these positions before the competition.
You must satisfy the market and await competition.
The competition may establish them first.
If they satisfy the market, don't try to copy them.
If they leave openings, you can go after them.

Some field positions give you a barricade.
I get to these positions before the enemy does.
You occupy their southern, sunny heights and wait for the
enemy.
Sometimes the enemy occupies these areas first.
If so, entice him away.
Never go after him.

Some field positions are too spread out.
Your force may seem equal to the enemy.
Still you will lose if you provoke a battle.
If you fight, you will not have any advantage.

These are the six types of field positions.
Each battleground has its own rules.
As a commander, you must know where to go.
You must examine each position closely.

Some armies can be outmaneuvered.
Some armies are too lax.
Some armies fall down.
Some armies fall apart.
Some armies are disorganized.
Some armies must retreat.

Know all six of these weaknesses.
They lead to losses on both good and bad ground.
They all arise from the army's commander.

Some market positions are easy to protect.
You must establish these positions before the competition.
You then must publicize your position and await
competitive attacks.
Sometimes the competition establishes these positions first.
If so, try to get them to muddy their position.
Do not attack competitors in these positions.

Some market positions are unfocused.
You may have sales and marketing equal to the competition.
Nevertheless, you are wasting your time trying to compete.
When you compete, these positions offer no advantage.

These are the six types of market positions.
Each marketplace has its own rules.
In marketing, you must know your position.
You must analyze each position carefully.

Some campaigns can be blunted.
Some campaigns are too bland.
Some campaigns stumble.
Some campaigns self-destruct.
Some campaigns are chaotic.
Some campaigns must be abandoned.

You must recognize these six weaknesses.
These problems arise in good and bad markets.
Your decisions create them.

One general can command a force equal to the enemy.
Still his enemy outflanks him.
This means that his army can be outmaneuvered.

Another can have strong soldiers, but weak officers.
This means that his army will be too lax.

Another has strong officers but weak soldiers.
This means that his army will fall down.

Another has sub-commanders that are angry and defiant.
They attack the enemy and fight their own battles.
As a commander, he cannot know the battlefield.
This means that his army will fall apart.

Another general is weak and easygoing.
He fails to make his orders clear.
His officers and men lack direction,
This shows in his military formations.
This means that his army will be disorganized.

Another general fails to predict the enemy.
He pits his small forces against larger ones.
He puts his weak forces against stronger ones.
He fails to pick his fights correctly.
This means that his army must retreat.

You must know all about these six weaknesses.
You must understand the philosophies that lead to defeat.
When a general arrives, you can know what he will do.
You must study each one carefully.

Your position may be equal to the competition.
Still, you let the competition twist your message.
This means that your campaign can be blunted.

Your sales force is good, but your message is weak.
This means that your campaign is too bland.

Your message is strong but your distribution is weak.
This means that your campaign will stumble.

Your sales managers are excitable and undisciplined.
They want to sell anyone they can find.
Then your company doesn't know its market.
This means that your campaign will self-destruct.

Some marketing is lazy and sloppy.
You fail to make your position clear.
Your marketing and sales lacks direction.
This shows in its lack of focus.
This means that your campaign is chaotic.

Some marketing fails to understand its competition.
You pit a weak message against a stronger one.
You pit a weak sales force against a stronger one.
You fail to pick your target market.
This means that your campaign must be abandoned.

You must understand all six of these faults.
You must understand the thinking that creates them.
When you face competition, you must know what to do.
You must study their faults carefully.

You must control your field position.
It will always strengthen your army.

You must predict the enemy to overpower him and win.
You must analyze the obstacles, dangers, and distances.
This is the best way to command.

Understand your field position before you go to battle.
Then you will win.
You can fail to understand your field position and still fight.
Then you will lose.

You must provoke battle when you will certainly win.
It doesn't matter what you are ordered.
The government may order you not to fight.
Despite that, you must always fight when you will win.

Sometimes provoking a battle will lead to a loss.
The government may order you to fight.
Despite that, you must avoid battle when you will lose.

You must advance without desiring praise.
You must retreat without fearing shame.
The only correct move is to preserve your troops.
This is how you serve your country.
This is how you reward your nation.

You must control your market position.
It must generate increased sales for your company.

You must foresee how to discredit the competition.
You must see the market's difficulties, problems, and needs.
This is the best way to campaign.

You must understand these issues when you campaign.
If you do, you will win your market.
You may not understand your market position.
Then you will lose your market.

You must attack a market when you know you will win it.
Forget your other priorities.
The company may not have planned on that market.
Still, you must campaign when the opportunity is there.

Sometimes, if you campaign you will lose the market.
Your company may desire that market.
Still, you must avoid campaigns that you will lose.

You must never campaign for the sake of pride.
Abandon failed campaigns without embarrassment.
The only goal is to increase your sales.
This is how you build your company.
This is how you ensure your success.

Think of your soldiers as little children.
You can make them follow you into a deep river.
Treat them as your beloved children.
You can lead them all to their deaths.

Some leaders are generous, but cannot use their men.
They love their men, but cannot command them.
Their men are unruly and disorganized.
These leaders create spoiled children.
Their soldiers are useless.

You may know what your soldiers will do in an attack.
You may not know if the enemy is vulnerable to attack.
You will then win only half the time.
You may know that the enemy is vulnerable to attack.
You may not know if your men are capable of attacking
them.
You will still win only half the time.
You may know that the enemy is vulnerable to attack.
You may know that your men are ready to attack.
You may not know how to position yourself in the field for
battle.
You will still win only half the time.

You must know how to make war.
You can then act without confusion.
You can attempt anything.

Think of your markets as your children.
They will support you in an unknown future.
Develop them with care and understanding.
They will serve you faithfully.

Some spend the money, but do not focus their markets.
If you care about your position, you must focus.
Otherwise, your campaign will be confused and sloppy.
You cannot be lax about focus.
Your marketing will be useless.

You can know that your product appeals to customers.
Nevertheless, you must know how to beat the competition.
If you don't, you have only done half of your job.
You can know how to beat the competition.
Nevertheless, you must also know that your product will appeal
to customers.
If you don't, you have only done half of your job.
You can know how to beat the competition.
You can know how to appeal to customers.
Nevertheless, you must also know exactly how to position
yourself in the campaign.
If you don't, you have done only half of your job.

You must know how to conduct a campaign.
You can then act with certainty.
You can market anything.

We say:
Know the enemy and know yourself.
Your victory will be painless.
Know the weather and the field.
Your victory will be complete.

❖

It is the old saying:
Know your competition and your market;
Then sales are effortless.
Understand customers' thinking and your position;
Then your success is assured.

Types of Terrain

Use the art of war.
Know when the terrain will scatter you.
Know when the terrain will be easy.
Know when the terrain will be disputed.
Know when the terrain is open.
Know when the terrain is intersecting.
Know when the terrain is dangerous.
Know when the terrain is bad.
Know when the terrain is confined.
Know when the terrain is deadly.

Warring parties must sometimes fight inside their own
territory.
This is scattering terrain.

When you enter hostile territory, your penetration is shallow.
This is easy terrain.

Some terrain gives me an advantageous position.
However, it gives others an advantageous position as well.
This will be disputed terrain.

MARKET CONDITIONS

Use your market sense:
Know when market conditions are tenuous.
Know when market conditions are easy.
Know when market conditions are contentious.
Know when market conditions are open.
Know when market conditions are shared.
Know when market conditions are serious.
Know when market conditions are bad.
Know when market conditions are restricting.
Know when market conditions are do-or-die.

You must sometimes defend against a new competitor in your established market.
This is a tenuous market.

When you start in a new market, your visibility is minimal.
This is an easy market.

Some market positions give you an advantage.
Nevertheless, competition can develop a good position as well.
This is a contentious market.

I can use some terrain to advance easily.
Others, however, can use it to move against me.
This is open terrain.

Everyone shares access to a given area.
The first one there can gather a larger group than anyone
else.
This is intersecting terrain.

You can penetrate deeply into hostile territory.
Then many hostile cities are behind you.
This is dangerous terrain.

There are mountain forests.
There are rugged hills.
There are marshes.
Everyone confronts these obstacles on a campaign.
They make bad terrain.

In some areas, the passage is narrow.
You are closed in as you enter and exit them.
In this type of area, a few people can attack our much larger
force.
This is confined terrain.

You can sometimes survive only if you fight quickly.
You will die if you delay.
This is deadly terrain.

You make easy progress in the market.
The competition, however, can still come in at any time.
This is an open market.

Several complementary companies sell to the same market.
The first to develop winning partnerships will dominate the market.
This is a shared market.

You invest heavily to develop a market.
The competition still has many devoted customers within it.
This is a serious market.

There are slow adopting market segments.
There are depressed market segments.
There are dying market segments.
Every company encounters these customers in marketing.
These are bad markets.

In some segments, the customer base is limited.
You are locked in once you win these markets.
A smaller, more specialized company can attack you within these markets.
These are restricting markets.

Sometimes you can win only if you commit all your resources.
Your will lose the market if you delay.
This is a do-or-die market.

To be successful, you control scattering terrain by not
fighting.
Control easy terrain by not stopping.
Control disputed terrain by not attacking.
Control open terrain by staying with the enemy's forces.
Control intersecting terrain by uniting with your allies.
Control dangerous terrain by plundering.
Control bad terrain by keeping on the move.
Control confined terrain by using surprise.
Control deadly terrain by fighting.

Go to any area that helps you in waging war.
You use it to cut off the enemy's contact between his front
and back lines.
Prevent his small parties from relying on his larger force.
Stop his strong divisions from rescuing his weak ones.
Prevent his officers from getting his men together.
Chase his soldiers apart to stop them from amassing.
Harass them to prevent their ranks from forming.

When joining battle gives you an advantage, you must do it.
When it isn't to your benefit, you must avoid it.

A daring soldier may ask:
"A large, organized enemy army and its general are coming.
What do I do to prepare for them?"

To be successful in tenuous markets, avoid encouraging competition.

In easy markets, don't stop campaigning.

In contentious markets, don't attack your competition.

In open markets, keep up with the competition.

In shared markets, make good alliances.

In serious markets, concentrate on closing sales.

In bad markets, get out and find another customer base.

In restricting markets, you must be inventive.

In do-or-die markets, fight to win.

Find the segments where you are the most competitive.

You must control the flow of information to customers about the marketplace.

Keep the competition from developing a foothold.

Keep your different competitors at odds with one another.

Prevent them from uniting against you.

Win away their customers to obstruct their growth.

Disrupt their distribution by stealing their channels.

When you have the advantage, force confrontations.

When you don't have the advantage, avoid confrontation.

You may ask:

"A large, well-organized competitor is coming into my market.
 What should I do?"

Tell him:
"First seize an area that the enemy must have.
Then they will pay attention to you.
Mastering speed is the essence of war.
Take advantage of a large enemy's inability to keep up.
Use a philosophy of avoiding difficult situations.
Attack the area where he doesn't expect you."

You must use the philosophy of an invader.
Invade deeply and then concentrate your forces.
This controls your men without oppressing them.

Get your supplies from the riches of the territory.
It is sufficient to supply your whole army.

Take care of your men and do not overtax them.
Your *esprit de corps* increases your momentum.
Keep your army moving and plan for surprises.
Make it difficult for the enemy to count your forces.
Position your men where there is no place to run.
They will then face death without fleeing.
They will find a way to survive.
Your officers and men will fight to their utmost.

Military officers that are completely committed lose their fear.
When they have nowhere to run, they must stand firm.
Deep in enemy territory, they are captives.
Since they cannot escape, they will fight.

There is an answer.
First, promote yourself as the leader in your segment.
Then the new competition must pay attention to you.
Inventing new issues quickly is the essence of a campaign.
Take advantage of a large competitor's inability to keep up.
Avoid battles over specific issues by shifting quickly.
Keep the discussion where the competition is unprepared.

You must have an aggressive marketing philosophy.
Commit totally to a segment and generate sales leads.
This commits your sales people without forcing them.

You must generate income quickly from the market.
Sales can pay for all your marketing efforts.

Take care of distribution channels and don't overburden them.
Share your company's success with your distributors.
Keep the marketing campaign moving and expect surprises.
Make it difficult for competition to understand your segment.
Put yourself in a position where you must dominate the segment.
You must bet everything on winning your target.
You will find a way to succeed.
Your sales people and distributors will support you.

When you commit yourself, you lose your fear of failure.
When you must win, you can stand your ground.
Committed to your target, you have no choice.
You will not look elsewhere; you will battle.

Commit your men completely.
Without being posted, they will be on guard.
Without being asked, they will get what is needed.
Without being forced, they will be dedicated.
Without being given orders, they can be trusted.

Stop them from guessing by removing all their doubts.
Stop them from dying by giving them no place to run.

Your officers may not be rich.
Nevertheless, they still desire plunder.
They may die young.
Nevertheless, they still want to live forever.

You must order the time of attack.
Officers and men may sit and weep until their lapels are wet.
When they stand up, tears may stream down their cheeks.
Put them in a position where they cannot run.
They will show the greatest courage under fire.

Make good use of war.
This demands instant reflexes.
You must develop these instant reflexes.
Act like an ordinary mountain snake.
Someone can strike at your head.
You can then attack with your tail.
Someone can strike at your tail.
You can then attack with your head.
Someone can strike at your middle.
You can then attack with both your head and tail.

Totally commit your organization to its customers.
Without being warned, everyone must be on guard.
Without being asked, everyone must do what is needed.
Without being forced, everyone must be dedicated.
Without being told, everyone must concentrate.

Stop any second-guessing by making your commitment clear.
Avoid failure by leaving them no excuses.

Your people and partners may not be rich.
This isn't because they don't want to win wealth.
You may all fail.
It shouldn't be because you didn't commit to success.

You must establish a date for total market commitment.
Everyone will complain and cry that they cannot meet it.
When they have to act, they will tell you that it's impossible.
Put them in a position where they have no choice.
They will find a way to make it work.

Make good use of your campaign.
Marketing demands quick reflexes.
Your must prepare to instantly overcome problems.
You should be able to act on instinct.
They will challenge your company's novelty.
Attack the competition for being laggards.
They will challenge you for being late.
Attack the competition for being hasty.
They can challenge you on any issue.
Immediately respond with attacks of your own.

A daring soldier asks:
"Can any army imitate these instant reflexes?"
We answer:
"It can."

To command and get the most of proud people, you must
study adversity.
People work together when they are in the same boat during
a storm.
In this situation, one rescues the other just as the right hand
helps the left.

Use adversity correctly.
Tether your horses and bury your wagon's wheels.
Still, you can't depend on this alone.
An organized force is braver than lone individuals.
This is the art of organization.
Put the tough and weak together.
You must also use the terrain.

Make good use of war.
Unite your men as one.
Never let them give up.

The commander must be a military professional.
This requires confidence and detachment.
You must maintain dignity and order.
You must control what your men see and hear.
They must follow you without knowing your plans.

You may question this.
Can you campaign using such aggressive responses?
There is only one answer.
You must!

To lead and control markets, you must understand how to use
market adversity.
You must bond with your market by accepting their problems as
your problems.
You will help each other when they realize that you are a partner
in their business.

Share your market's worries.
Tie your future together with theirs.
Even this isn't enough.
True partners are more courageous than lone companies.
This is the art of collaborating.
You must help your weakest customers the most.
You must use your market leverage.

Make good use of campaigning.
Unite with your customers.
You must never give up on them.

ふーく

You must be a marketing professional.
This requires confidence and detachment.
You must maintain your leadership and focus.
You must control what your customer sees and hears.
They must believe you without knowing your plans.

You can reinvent your men's roles.
You can change your plans.
You can use your men without their understanding.

You must shift your campgrounds.
You must take detours from the ordinary routes.
You must use your men without giving them your strategy.

A commander provides what his army needs now.
You must be willing to climb high and then kick away your
ladder.
You must be able to lead your men deeply into your enemy's
territory and then find a way to create the opportunity that
you need.

You must drive men like a flock of sheep.

You must drive them to march.
You must drive them to attack.
You must never let them know where you are headed.
You must unite them into a great army.
You must then drive them against all opposition.
This is the job of a true commander.

You must adapt to the different terrain.
You must adapt to find an advantage.
You must manage your people's affections.
You must study all these skills.

You must reinvent market definitions.
You can change your focus.
You must lead because you have more knowledge.

You must change your tactics.
You must create new distribution channels.
The market should never anticipate you.

You must provide exactly what is needed at the moment.
You must be willing to go out on a limb and take a risk on a market.
You must get deeply involved with your customers to find the problems that create the opportunities that you need to win them over.

You must inspire customers to act together.

You must compel them to throw away the old.
You must entice them to try something new.
You must never let them take you for granted.
You must unite your sales resource into a great force.
You must dominate all competition.
This is the job of a true market leader.

You must adapt to every market condition.
You must adjust your methods to win customers.
You must play on a market's emotions.
You must learn all these skills.

Always use the philosophy of invasion.
Deep invasions concentrate your forces.
Shallow invasions scatter your forces.
When you leave your country and cross the border, you must
take control.
This is always critical ground.
You can sometimes move in any direction.
This is always intersecting ground.
You can penetrate deeply into a territory.
This is always dangerous ground.
You penetrate only a little way.
This is always easy ground.
Your retreat is closed and the path ahead tight.
This is always confined ground.
There is sometimes no place to run.
This is always deadly ground.

To use scattering terrain correctly, we must inspire our men's
devotion.
On easy terrain, we must keep in close communication.
On disputed terrain, we should try to hamper the enemy's
progress.
On open terrain, we must carefully defend our chosen
position.
On intersecting terrain, we must solidify our alliances.
On dangerous terrain, we must ensure our food supplies.
On bad terrain, we must keep advancing along the road.
On confined terrain, we must barricade a stronghold on the
high ground.
On deadly terrain, we must show what we can do by killing
the enemy.

You must always campaign aggressively.
Commitment to a segment focuses your efforts.
Weak commitments dissipate your resources.
When you commit yourself to a customer base, you must take leadership.
This is a critical time.
When you can choose your channels,
Create good partnerships.
If you devote yourself to a competitor's market,
This is always a serious situation.
When you first enter a promising market,
This is always the easy part of the campaign.
If the market has only a few key customers,
These are restricting market conditions.
If you must win a segment immediately,
This is a do-or-die situation.

To succeed in tenuous markets, you must earn your customer's devotion.
In easy markets, you must meet often with customers.
In contentious markets, your must create obstacles for your competitors.
In open markets, you must defend your position and your proposal.
In shared markets, you must join your partners.
In serious markets, you must have plenty of resources.
In bad markets, you must find a new type of customer.
In restricting markets, you must defend your position with top customers.
In do-or-die markets, you must prove yourself by dominating the competition.

Make your men feel like an army.
Surround them and they will defend themselves.
If they cannot avoid it, they will fight.
If they are under pressure, they will obey.

Do the right thing when you don't know your different
enemies' plans.
Don't attempt to meet them.

You don't know the local mountains, forests, hills and
marshes?
Then you cannot march the army.
You don't have local guides?
You won't get any of the benefits of the terrain.

There are many factors in war.
You may lack knowledge of any one of them.
If so, it is wrong to take a nation into war.

You must be able to dominate a nation at war.
Divide a big nation before they are able to gather a large
force.
Increase your enemy's fear.
Prevent his forces from getting together and organizing.

Do the right thing and don't try to compete for outside
alliances.
You won't have to fight for authority.
Trust only yourself and your own resources.
This increases the enemy's uncertainty.
You can force one of his allies to pull out.
His whole nation can fall.

Make your team powerful.
If they are committed, they will succeed.
When they have no choice, they will work.
When they are pressured, they will follow your lead.

☷——★

Do the right thing when you don't understand the competition's position.
Don't try to attack their market.

If you don't understand the target customer's buying habits, tastes and needs,
Then you cannot start a marketing campaign.
If you don't hire people who know the market,
You won't know the market's thinking or needs.

There is so much to know in marketing.
You don't want to miss anything.
Otherwise, you can't control the results of the campaign.

You must pressure large competitors in your market.
Steal away their ideas and momentum before they can establish a foothold.
Increase their disappointment in the market.
Prevent them from developing partners and an organization.

Do the right thing and don't always depend on partners to help with every market.
Then you won't have to fight for leadership.
Trust yourself and your own resources.
This decreases the competition's source of information.
You may convince your competitors' allies to abandon them.
Their whole campaign may then collapse.

119

Distribute plunder without worrying about agreements.
Halt without the government's command.
Attack with the whole strength of your army.
Use your army as if it was a single man.

Attack with skill.
Do not discuss it.
Attack when you have an advantage.
Do not talk about the dangers.
When you can launch your army into deadly ground, even if
it stumbles, it can still survive.
You can be weakened in a deadly battle and yet be stronger
afterward.

Even a large force can fall into misfortune.
If you fall behind, however, you can still turn defeat into
victory.
You must use the skills of war.
To survive, you must adapt to your enemy's purpose.
You must stay with him no matter where he goes.
It may take a thousand miles to kill the general.
If you correctly understand him, you can find the skill to do
it.

Manage your government correctly at the start of a war.
Close your borders and tear up passports.
Block the passage of envoys.
Encourage politicians at headquarters to stay out of it.
You must use any means to put an end to politics.
Your enemy's people will leave you an opening.
You must instantly invade through it.

Working alone, you don't play politics.
You can change your offerings without discussion.
You can focus all your resources on the target customer.
You can work with a single goal.

Campaign with skill.
Don't expose your plans.
Be aggressive when you find an edge.
Don't advertise the risks.
You can get into bad markets and lose customers, but you can still survive.
You may lose ground in a competitive battle, but you can also learn from your mistakes.

You can win many times and still get into bad situations.
If you make mistakes, you can still turn initial failure into ultimate success.
You must use your marketing skills.
In marketing, you must adapt completely to market conditions.
You must stay with the competition no matter where they go.
You can turn customers around and overturn a market leader.
If you understand the competition, you can find a way to beat them.

Do the right things at the start of a campaign.
Protect existing markets and keep the competition out.
Prevent your plans from leaking.
Get the complete commitment of company management.
Eliminate anything that disturbs your focus.
Learn the competition's weaknesses.
Quickly take advantage of them.

Immediately seize a place that they love.
Do it quickly.
Trample any border to pursue the enemy.
Use your judgment about when to fight.

Doing the right thing at the start of war is like approaching a
woman.
Your enemy's men must open the door.
After that, you should act like a streaking rabbit.
The enemy will be unable to catch you.

Quickly seize a key customer base in the market.
Waste no time.
Change the market's definition and attack the competition.
Use your best judgement about where to compete.

Success at the beginning comes from wooing target customers
like a woman.
The competition will eventually leave you an opening.
After that, you should act quickly and unpredictably.
The competition will be unable to catch up with you.

Attacking with Fire

There are five ways of attacking with fire.
The first is burning troops.
The second is burning supplies.
The third is burning supply transport.
The fourth is burning storehouses.
The fifth is burning camps.

To make fire, you must have the resources.
To build a fire, you must prepare the raw materials.

To attack with fire, you must be in the right season.
To start a fire, you must have the time.

Choose the right season.
The weather must be very dry.

Choose the right time.
Pick a season when the grass is as high as the side of a cart.

You can tell the proper days by the stars in the night sky.
You want days when the wind rises in the morning.

TARGETING MARKET DESIRES

There are five categories of market desires:
The first is the need for safety.
The second is the need for comfort.
The third is the need for pride.
The fourth is the need to for gain.
The fifth is the need for affection.

To address market needs, you must offer unique value.
To stimulate desire, you must know the market's thinking.

To target a need, your customer base must feel it.
To create a desire, you must take your time.

Understand your market's seasons.
Campaign when the customer has time to buy.

Be careful of your timing.
Pick a time when your target has plenty of money.

To know the right time, analyze your market's news.
You want to pick a time when pressure is building.

Everyone attacks with fire.
You must create five different situations with fire and be able
to adjust to them.

You start a fire inside the enemy's camp.
Then attack the enemy's periphery.

You launch a fire attack, but the enemy remains calm.
Wait and do not attack.

The fire reaches its height.
Follow its path if you can.
If you can't follow it, stay where you are.

Spreading fires on the outside of camp can kill.
You can't always get fire inside the enemy's camp.
Take your time in spreading it.

Set the fire when the wind is at your back.
Don't attack into the wind.
Daytime winds last a long time.
Night winds fade quickly.

Every army must know how to deal with the five attacks by
fire.
Use many men to guard against them.

Everyone tries to address market needs.
You must respond to the five types of desire and adjust to your competition's approach.

You can target a need central to the competition's position.
Then you start stealing away their outlying customers.

You may target a need that doesn't concern the market.
Wait to build desire before you start campaigning.

Some market needs demand attention now.
Present solutions immediately if you can.
If you can't address these issues, wait for a better time.

Publicizing new issues can win markets.
Many times, you can't attack the competition's issues.
Take your time spreading your new viewpoint.

You can fan market desires.
Don't fight against prevailing attitudes.
Well-publicized needs get attention.
Less visible needs are easily overlooked.

You must master these five approaches to attacking market desires.
You defend your segment by guarding against them.

When you use fire to assist your attacks, you are being
clever.
Water can add force to an attack.
You can also use water to disrupt an enemy.
It doesn't, however, take his resources.

You win in battle by getting the opportunity to attack.
It is dangerous if you fail to study how to accomplish this
achievement.
As commander, you cannot waste your opportunities.

We say:
A wise leader plans success.
A good general studies it.
If there is little to be gained, don't act.
If there is little to win, do not use your men.
If there is no danger, don't fight.

As leader, you cannot let your anger interfere with the
success of your forces.
As commander, you cannot fight simply because you are
enraged.
Join the battle only when it is in your advantage to act.
If there is no advantage in joining a battle, stay put.

Anger can change back into happiness.
Rage can change back into joy.
A nation once destroyed cannot be brought back to life.
Dead men do not return to the living.

Leveraging market desires to generate sales is smart marketing.
Using the media can add force to your campaign.
You can use the media to hurt the competition's sales.
Media alone, however, doesn't generate sales.

8━━☆

You win markets by leveraging your strengths.
It is a mistake not to concentrate your campaign on your real competence.
In marketing, you cannot waste any opportunity.

This much is true.
If you are smart, you plan to win target customers.
If you are clever, you examine past successes.
If the segment isn't worth the effort, don't target it.
If it can't be profitable, don't waste your resources.
If the target customers lack real desire, don't sell to them.

You must never let your emotions affect the success of your marketing.
You must never go after a segment simply because it excites you.
Do only what is needed to make progress.
If you don't belong in a market, stay out of it.

A weak market can change to a good one.
Pride can be easily humbled.
If you lose a customer base, you will not get it back.
Worthless markets cannot make you successful.

This fact must make a wise leader cautious.
A good general is on guard.

Your philosophy must be to keep the nation peaceful and the army intact.

Knowing this, you must be selective.
You must always be on watch for the best opportunities.

Your plan must be to pick the right new customers and protect existing markets.

Using Spies

Altogether, building an army requires thousands of men.
They invade and march thousands of miles.
Whole families are destroyed.
Other families must be heavily taxed.
Every day, thousands of dollars must be spent.

Internal and external events force people to move.
They are unable to work while on the road.
They are unable to find and hold a useful job.
This affects seventy percent of thousands of families.

You can watch and guard for years.
Then a single battle can determine victory in a day.
Despite this, bureaucrats hold onto their salary money too
dearly.
They remain ignorant of the enemy's condition.
The result is cruel.

They are not leaders of men.
They are not servants of the state.
They are not masters of victory.

Using Research

Building a market requires many resources.
You have to make thousands of contacts.
This requires months of time.
The company must pay for your efforts.
Every day, marketing consumes money.

Internal and external issues consume your people's time.
This time is wasted if it doesn't win customers.
People do not necessarily know what is productive.
This confusion can eat away most of your resources.

You can develop and protect your markets for years.
You can lose them in a single day.
Despite this, many marketing people spend their budgets on staff salaries.
You cannot afford to stay ignorant of market conditions.
The result is devastating.

Without information, you cannot dominate a segment.
You can not support your company.
You cannot be successful.

You need a creative leader and a worthy commander.
You must move your troops to the right places to beat
others.
You must accomplish your attack and escape unharmed.
This requires foreknowledge.
You can obtain foreknowledge.
You can't get it from demons or spirits.
You can't see it from professional experience.
You can't check it with analysis.
You can only get it from other people.
You must always know the enemy's situation.

You must use five types of spies.
You need local spies.
You need inside spies.
You need double agents.
You need doomed spies.
You need surviving spies.

You need all five types of spies.
No one must discover your methods.
You will be then able to put together a true picture.
This is the commander's most valuable resource.

You need local spies.
Get them by hiring people from the countryside.

You need inside spies.
Win them by subverting government officials.

You need double agents.
Discover enemy agents and convert them.

You must be an inventive and valuable leader.
You must spend your resources in the right places to win markets.
You must attack new segments without risking damage.
This requires information.
You can get this information.
You won't get it from theory.
You won't get it from past experience.
You can't reason it out.
You can only get it by asking people questions.
You must always know your market's thinking.

There are only five types of research.
There is research on the target customer.
There is research on your competition.
There is research on distribution channels.
There is research on the products themselves.
There is research on specific customers.

You must use all five types of research.
If you do, no one will ever challenge your knowledge.
You can learn about any market and its workings.
This information is your most valuable resource.

You need information on your target customers.
Win it by hiring experts from within the marketplace.

You need information on the competition.
Find competing sales people and hire them away.

You need information on distribution channels.
Find the competition's distributors and win them over.

You need doomed spies.
Deceive professionals into being captured.
We let them know our orders.
They then take those orders to our enemy.

You need surviving spies.
Someone must return with a report.

Your job is to build a complete army.
No relations are as intimate as they are with spies.
No rewards are too generous for spies.
No work is as secret as that of spies.

If you aren't clever and wise, you can't use spies.
If you aren't fair and just, you can't use spies.
If you can't see the tiny subtleties, you won't get the truth
from spies.

Pay attention to small, trifling details!
Spies are helpful in every area.

Spies are the first to hear information, so they must not
spread it.
Spies who give your location or talk to others must be killed
along with those to whom they have talked.

You need information on specific products.
Find a way to buy or access those products or their users.
Spend the time to discover their weaknesses.
Mislead the competition about your products.

You need information about specific customers.
Get it from the customers themselves.

Your job is to develop a strong market.
No resources are as critical as information sources.
No reward is too generous for good information.
No knowledge is as confidential as your research.

You must be bright and perceptive to correlate data.
You must be open and unbiased to evaluate information.
If you aren't sensitive to subtleties, you won't find the truth
in research.

You must pay close attention to small details.
Research is helpful in every area.

Your market research gathers information but it must not
spread it.
Research that divulges your plans or position to the
competition can destroy you.

You may want to attack an army's position.
You may want to attack a certain fortification.
You may want to kill people in a certain place.
You must first know the guarding general.
You must know his left and right flanks.
You must know his hierarchy.
You must know the way in.
You must know where different people are stationed.
We must demand this information from our spies.

I want to know the enemy spies in order to convert new spies into my men.
You find a source of information and bribe them.
You must bring them in with you.
You must obtain them as double agents and use them as your emissaries.

Do this correctly and carefully.
You can contact both local and inside spies and obtain their support.
Do this correctly and carefully.
You create doomed spies by deceiving professionals.
You can use them to give false information.
Do this correctly and carefully.
You must have surviving spies capable of bringing you information at the right time.

You may want to address a competitor's position.
You may want to go after specific customers.
You may want to win a certain target market.
You must first know how competing executives think.
You must know the extent of their market penetration.
You must know their organization.
You must know what weaknesses you can exploit.
You must know who their workers are.
You must get this information from your research.

You want to know who does the research for your
competition and hire them.
You must be willing to pay for information.
You must win market contacts over to your side.
You must win the existing channels over to become your
distributors.

You must do this carefully.
You can hire from within a market and the competition and
get their knowledge.
You must also do this selectively.
You can discover product information from users.
You can use their insight into the competition's thinking.
You must do this quietly as well.
You need detailed information on specific customers at the
appropriate time.

These are the five different types of intelligence work.
You must be certain to master them all.
You must be certain to create double agents.
You cannot afford to be too cheap in creating these double agents.

This technique created the success of ancient emperors.
This is how they held their dynasties.

You must always be careful of your success.
Learn from the past examples.

Be a smart commander and good general.
You do this by using your best and brightest people for spying.
This is how you achieve the greatest success.
This is how you meet the necessities of war.
The whole army's position and ability to move depends on these spies.

There are five different types of research.
You must be certain to master them all.
You must be certain to understand distribution.
You cannot invest too much time understanding market channels.

&—★

This is how companies have been successful in marketing.
This is how they have built commercial empires.

You must always be subtle in your campaigning.
Learn from the history of past success.

You must be an informed and capable market leader.
You must use your best and brightest people to gather information.
This is how you achieve the greatest success.
This is how you satisfy the needs of the market.
Your marketing position and ability to attack new segments depend on research.

💰 💰 💰

The Original Text

Sun Tzu originally wrote his text in Chinese characters. Any English translation is only an approximation of Sun Tzu's words. However, we want to make it easy to read and appreciate Sun Tzu's text in its original form. *The Art of War: In Sun Tzu's Own Words* offers Sun Tzu's Chinese text as he originally wrote it with a character-by-character and line-by-line translation into English.

This book contains two complete works. It contains Sun Tzu's original characters translated one at a time in the phrases he actually used. It also offers the *The Art of War* translated line-by-line into everyday English. The two versions are shown side-by-side to complete a picture of the Sun Tzu's original lessons on warfare.

The Art of War: In Sun Tzu's Own Words
ISBN: 19291940015
Paperback. $9.95.

Clearbridge Publishing's books may be purchased for business, for any promotional use or for special sales. Please contact:
Clearbridge Publishing

Phone: (206) 533-9357
Fax: (206) 546-9756
Mail: P.O. Box 7055, Shoreline, WA 98133
E-mail: info@clearbridge.com.
Web: www.clearbridge.com

For Sales Professionals

The Art of Marketing addresses the strategic issues of competing for markets. We want to make it easy to apply the competitive lessons of *The Art of War* to the needs of individual sales people fighting for orders. *The Art of War & The Art of Sales* takes Sun Tzu's lessons and applies them specifically to today's problems of contacting customers, convincing them and winning their on-going business.

This book also contains two complete works. It contains Gagliardi's basic translation of *The Art of War*. Additionally, it offers the ideas of *The Art of War* interpreted line-by-line for working sales professionals. Any sales manager or company president would be happy with the results if they could get their sales people to follow Sun Tzu's advice. The enemy is the competition. The battleground is the customer's mind. Victory is winning an on-going relationship with the customer. The two versions are shown side-by-side to complete the picture of the Sun Tzu approach to modern selling.

The Art of War & The Art of Sales
ISBN: 1929194013
Paperback. $14.95.

Clearbridge Publishing's books may be purchased for business, for any promotional use or for special sales. Please contact:

Clearbridge Publishing
Phone: (206) 533-9357
Fax: (206) 546-9756
Mail: P.O. Box 7055, Shoreline, WA 98133
E-mail: info@clearbridge.com
Web: www.clearbridge.com